The Thirteenth Circle

A Confessional

Chaz Allen

Copyright © 2019 Chaz Allen McQuerrey

All rights reserved. This book or any portion thereof may not be reproduced or used in any manner whatsoever without the express written permission of the publisher except for the use of brief quotations in a book review.

Printed in the United States of America

Library of Congress Control Number: 2021903749

First Edition/First Printing, 2019

Cover and Illustration:

Ignacio Paul - nachoandrespaul.myportfolio.com

ISBN: 978-0-578-62801-1

For inquiries regarding quantity orders, permission requests or any related information, please submit a contact form via the link below:

www.ChazAllenArt.com/reachout

*This book is dedicated to my mother, sister, and father.
To our story, and to the impact I hope to make through it.*

Author Testimony

"I want this book to be something people read and resonate with. I don't want people to feel sorry for me, dwell on the details shared, think I'm just whining, or spend too much time trying to decipher anything; it may take a few times around for that. I want people to understand It's much bigger than me. Like many before, I want this to be an example for all who have struggled. It's meant to show how they can overcome; that it is possible."

"These are ongoing issues that exist in all communities around the world. I didn't write this as an attempt to convey some sort of unjust mistreatment by life, but to bring to light issues so many people face and never find a way out of. This is just the beginning and I'm quite anxious to see how people respond. I hope I'm able to utilize this for much more going forward, but regardless, there is more work to come, more refined work. I'll always be a writer, no matter what."

Table of Contents

Prologue	1
3am	2
Birth:Death	3
Bound	4
Butterfly	5
Cataclysm	6
Catch and Release	7
Celestial	8
CHI	9
Climb	10
Courage	11
Dark Matter	12
Day 3	13
Descendant	14
Destiny	15
Deus	16
Discovery	17
Emotion	18
Epiphany	19
Epitome	20
Faith	21
Future	22
Gatekeeper	23
Growth	24
Hell	25
I'm Sure	26
Identity	27
Image of a Ghost	28
Indignation	29
It Breeds	30
Kings	31
Love	32
Mind	33
Missing Her	34
Moonlight	35

Mother	36
Once	37
Pandora	38
Peace	39
Posterity	40
Prairie	41
Puppet Master	42
Purgatory	43
Purpose	44
Rain	45
River	46
Salvation	47
Singularity	48
Sorry	49
Succession	50
Suicide	51
The Brotherhood	52
The Good Shepard	53
The Grey	54
The Less You Say	55
The Marker Ones	56
The Skelton Key	57
The Voyage	58
Time	59
Tomorrow	60
Transmigration	61
Twelve	62
Veil	63
Vessels	64
Void	65
Wave	66
You Should Rest	67
Epilogue	68

TRIGGER WARNING

This book contains sensitive subject matter and imagery that some readers may find controversial.

Certain themes discussed involve: Prostitution, Drug Use, Suicide, and Abortion.

Images depicted are original works that some may perceive as dark and/or violent in nature.

-Prologue-

"Welcome and thank you for taking the time to be here with me today. This is a factual account of my early life. This work represents many facets of that life and me as an individual. Some of which stemmed from moments of insanity, moments of joy, of heartbreak, depression, euphoria, and everything in between."

"I've chosen to share this collection of work because of a deeply seeded need to express a greater message. Some of these pieces you may not fully understand and that's perfectly fine. Quite frankly, I don't understand all of them myself. Study and discern them if you wish. I'll do my best to walk you through my journey thus far. I only ask that you do not hold judgment against me and mine."

"My name is Chaz Allen, and at the time of writing this, I'm 26 years old. I've been fortunate and blessed enough to experience many great things thus far, as well as many bad. I'm a man of many interests and passions, much to the likes of most."

"One thing I know for certain is that I am a writer. It's just about the only thing I've ever done for no reason at all. Well, no other reason than to express an idea. Therefore, I'd like to make this book a walk with you. A conversation if you will, between you and me. I'm going to start at an early point with you. We'll talk about what some of these poems mean, as well as what inspired them. I look forward to discussing these with you. Let's begin..."

3 a.m.

I met an angel;
she spoke in the most beautiful of voices.

Birth:Death

A plain of which none know,
to a point of singularity;
the rays wound tight to transmit.

The cusp of all we hold dear,
shaping our deliverance from frailty.

Across eons we collide
with a weighted purpose.

Neither forward nor back.
The Majestic incarnate,
in what has always been.

Do not despair,
for I have always known you.
Our encapsulation begins
when we meet at the horizon.

Bound

There will be a reason
I call to you this day.
You're fate entwined
with infernal offerings,
summons me to this cause.

Could you relent to me?
Would you dare answer?
Would I understand the question?

The shroud remains sewn.
The Thirteenth Cycle deemed it so;
His act was written.

I've gazed in His direction.
He adverted me to you.
I know his will.
He cares not of my sacrifice.
For one day,
I shall come to know.

Butterfly

There you sit
perched on my sill,
and yet,
you've eluded me.

Why should you return,
that I may merely observe?

I aim to grasp
but am met with breeze
from your wings.

To the fields
and forests you go.

You've eluded me.

The moons luminance
casts radiance upon you,
perched on my sill.

My chin rests upon my hands;
eyes fixated on your dance.

I dare not grasp,
for to the fields
and forests you go.

I shall call you,

sleep.

Cataclysm

How frail the mind becomes
when it must accept,
it cannot control their voices.

It is I,
who release and relinquish
these binds. The veil of their
encumbrance evermore removed.

The hourglass is fleeting
as I stand aside it watching,
waiting for the light of the sun.

The structure has been rebuilt.
We stand on the first plank
looking onward,
hoping it survives the storm.

"Cataclysm" was one of many pieces I've written, about the "voices" I often tell people these poems come from. I know when I say that I must sound schizophrenic. It's much deeper than that, however, as any creative must "hear" or "see". Many times, the words that are subsequently written, do start as a mere flow of dialogue through my head."

Catch & Release

Again — the door ~~frozen~~.
Last,
there was no answer.

I walk through —   { I cross
Dust behind;   I enter
Stain hath followed.

Forgive me.

Catch & Release

Again –
The Door.

Last,
there was no answer.

I cross –
dust behind;
stain hath followed.

Forgive Me.

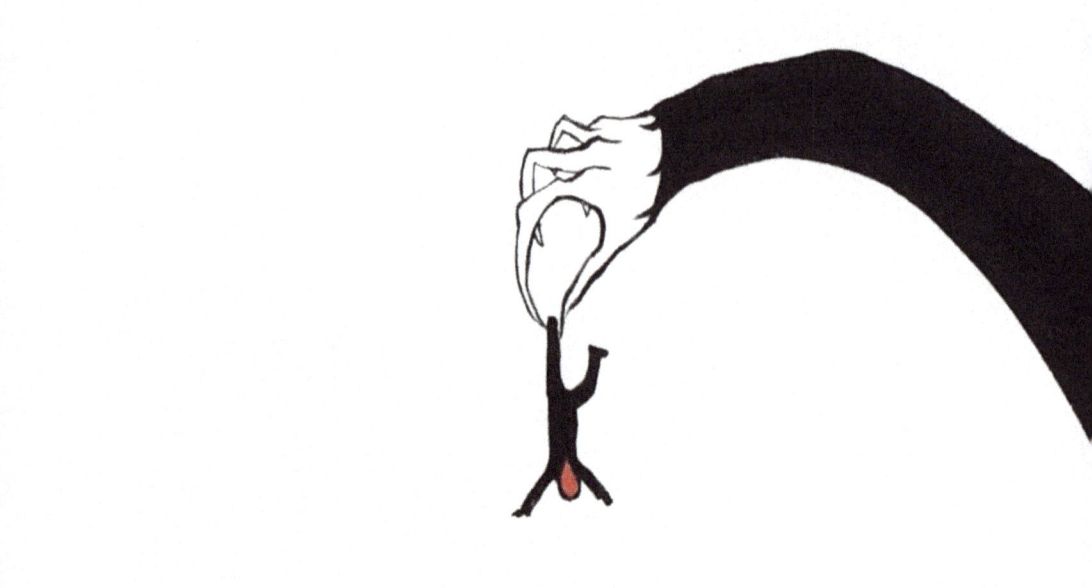

Celestial

Know young one,
I will not soon forget you.
Your transcendent energy
shall reassemble, as you
continue in eclectic dwelling.

Understand through this,
your prowess has been
strengthened and solidified.

Your reincarnation
has been written to prosper.
I'll pass by you one day.
You'll have risen
greater than I could have known.

As I had only begun to learn;
His grace will touch us both,
for only a moment.

"Celestial" represents something very personal to me and one of my greatest regrets in life. When I was younger, I ended up in a position of unwanted pregnancy. I received a call from the young woman I was with and was told. I don't think it was coincidence that it happened in the middle of a fight either. I was infuriated and in shock all at once. Ultimately though, I knew I was not ready to be a father. I barely knew how to be a man. So, I forced her to have an abortion."

"Well, forced is probably a strong way of putting it; close, however. We both knew the situation we were in. We awoke early one summer morning and made the two-hour drive to have the procedure. A few hours later, and five hundred dollars spent, we were no longer parents. Though it was extremely difficult to do, in the end, we knew it was for the best."

"I vividly remember us walking back to my car after we left the clinic; she was crying by now. There was a brown paper bag on the floorboard of my car. I don't recall whether or not we planned to have it, but it was thoroughly used. She threw up the entire trip back home. I dwelled on what had transpired for days, even weeks afterward. The guilt wasn't an easy pill to swallow and its repression has been necessary. I'm still not ready for a child even now and wouldn't know what to do if I fell into a similar situation again.".

"I worry a coward would prevail. Then again, through rigorous trial since, perhaps not. This piece was to commemorate the seed that I had given life and hence, had taken away."

A movement amidst
the ~~scribbled~~
ripples; Reflective
op the paradigm.

~~scribbled~~
Such an Intrinsic
placement of
motion. ~~scribbled~~

The essence of
our heavenly
body, suspended
in calamity of
touch and ~~scribbled~~ release.

A sap
over the
receding,
glance through
the visible ~~scribbled~~ spectrum.
ble
waves collide
through ~~the~~ the ~~scribbled~~
vibrations. ethers.

To the eyes of the
master; To the neck
of the apprentice.
Our malevolence ~~scribbled~~
~~scribbled~~ embraced by
compassionate word.

other ~~scribbled~~ ~~scribbled~~
~~scribbled~~ the blade
has reciprocated here,

CHI

A movement amidst the ripple,
reflective of the paradigm.

Such an intrinsic
placement of motion.

The essence
of our heavenly body,
suspended in the calamity
of catch and release.

To the eyes of the Master;
to the heart of the apprentice.

Our malevolence
embraced by compassionate word.

A step after the preceding;
a glance through the visible spectrum.

Inaudible waves collide
through the ether's vibration.

Whether the blade
has reverberated here,
it has surely cut there.

I have to —
have to.

From the place I've come

to

the place I'm going.

I have to.

If only you could know — only see.

have

Climb

I have to —
I have to.

From the place I've come,
to the place I'm going.

I

H
A
V
E

T
O

If you could only know —
only see.

I have to.

"*I place a lot of pressure on myself in almost everything I do. For me, it's nearly impossible not to. Though, it is certainly important to keep this in check. "Climb" is for those with relentless self-demand.*"

Courage

Oh, what a looming scream,
rippled through the cast
of the soldering blade.

Of heroic tasks
the elders have made.

The pursuit is unknown,
as we stand tall and alone.
Perhaps a screech or a moan,
what a price we must pay.

A darkened glimpse,
of all failed attempts.
To enlighten a gaze
of where not, we shall stay.

Complacent creatures,
with such burning desire.
These jobs have been chosen,
there's a coward for hire.

Appeased is not
the soldering blade,
for it must remain pierced,
to step out of the grave.

Dark Matter

He has heard it once,
we are primordial sound.

These intricacies of being.
The complexity of what's been woven,
never knowing as we sway.

Pleading,
as motion threatens to leave us.
Light is to dark, as dark is to light.

Such maddening scenes of sacrament
that bellow from below.
Those souls lost,
who plead for redemption;
this light does not grace thee.

One's realization of self
leads ever closer to the fault of sanity.

Pillars of hope
must bleed amongst these materials
to create our physical matter.
Vile as it may be,
you must be able to see the sun.

Day 3

Ah! Yes!

Here it is —
right through this door.

The mess has been cleaned,
you see!?

Not a drop on the floor.

That'll do my dear,
we can't risk it again.

Away we must go —
mere scuff on the chin.

But oh!

What a beautiful sight it was
my wonderful spouse.

How I do wish,
we weren't missing the house.

Descendant

With the power you claim,
you must know the peril
of our divided bloodline.

You spoke with a whisper
and tore me in two.
One's wisdom extends
only until they realize
they have none.

How shall a descendant
march toward the light?
Should he follow bulb or candle?

Your quarrel
has left us here to ponder;
to bear the weight
of bickering children.

Once we choose to remove
the chains from each arm
and the veil from thine eye,
how do we accept and embrace
darkness; the light.

Perhaps
we are all doomed to wander,
till' we have found the door
and received the word.

"It's always driven me crazy how we've been placed here in the duality of our world. We've been preached to and sold so many variations of a story, that quite frankly, no one knows. At-least if they do, they aren't sharing all of it with us. I wanted to express that struggle here, between God and the Devil that is. We're merely caught in the middle. A constant pull back and forth while these deities bicker and battle."

"The human struggle and our need to find purpose, is never far from where one feels they come from; what they're truly connected to. Some people choose upright paths that are respectable in this search and others, not so much. Rather, quite the opposite. Either way, the crux of our existence ever rests in the middle."

Destiny

I've seen the wolf
amidst the village.
He travels with the moon
and holds an image
of the Island in his head.

There are remnants
upon his name as the day breaks.

He sees clearly at night
and retains due process
of the lessons his Master's
taught him.

To his eyes one must gaze.
With the affliction of his
teaching, pain must be
bared; sheep shall perish.

There is no village
where he may place claim.
The Island requires he learn to swim.

Deus

The whirlwind voices
of the masquerade.

A scream from oceans wind,
to settled breezes through a sill.

A dawns ancient ray;
birth to the silence.

The mystery of the night.
Darkness as deep
as the depths of the soul.

The dreams of what's further.
Expanded perceptions embrace
counterparts to entwine.

The warmest hours solace.
Steady true; calm and quiet,
as you were meant to be.

Discovery

The journey of the self-righteous
man exists as a lone wanderer.
Along dirt roads, amidst the beasts
of our Mother's beauty and rage.

Solemnly riddled by plague
of constructed foundations,
epitomizing scattered dismemberment.

Sunken soles into a wet earths
puddle reflecting I,
the self-righteous man,
gazing down upon the earth
revered, with eyes of holy fire
and vengeance.

The Son's glory be upon you.

Emotion

I answered no;
the paper kept them when I released the pen.

Epiphany

Oh yes,
I had a dream.

A dream of
what death would be.

— the scariest thing.

Then I realized,
that would be the moment;
the most beautiful moment.

Given unto you
what you've always
asked for.

— His voice.

So beautiful,
that your cries will be deafening
as you re-enter the world.

Reduced to what you once were,
ready to begin again.

Epitome

Why has the gaze
been placed upon the ants?

Universes aligned,
understand and acknowledge
a greater cause.

Should one expect
such splendor
from a hill of sand?

Intentions rest to wash it away,
and yet, we call to you.

There is fog with dawn;
a haze with dusk.

You rest between.

Understand what you create.
It exists as a parable of reason.
Know this as we speak,
I've longed for your voice.

Those around me are as feeble
as what we've constructed here.

"Epitome", yet again, questions what God expects of us knowing how easily we are led astray. There are numerous cultures with varied beliefs, all searching for meaning and fulfillment in something more. What do you believe God expects of us? Who is he/she/it to you?"

Faith

It is a stalk
amidst the very many,
that sways a friendly
greeting toward you.

This stalk, however,
is different.

It is a single stalk.
It stands and sways
as the others do.

Yet,
this stalk is different.

The stalk I speak of
is not a legend.
I implore you to find it.
For if you do,
a bountiful meal is provided
every night of the year,
forever.

This stalk plays no tricks
for those who seek it.
It makes no attempt to hide.

Sometimes,
if you listen very closely,
you can hear it calling to you.

If you befriend this stalk,
you mustn't let it go.

You must cherish it,
for it will keep you full,
and you will let it.

It is a stalk
amidst the very many.

This stalk, however,
is different.

If you find it,
please do let me know.

I seem to keep losing mine.

Future

The future speaks to me
as a brisk wind,
clashing and fleeting
with whispers and hints.
Knowing me better than I,
pushing as I remain still.

I remain filled with the
limitlessness of the universe.
My aspirations of an
internal power manifested.
The paths remain numerous
and bound to choice.

They call it a jungle;
we plant many trees.
The devastation of the
mind and decision,
force me to ensure many grow.

The future has not waited
and motion has nearly given up on me.
Clouds clear with voices
of certainty and resolve.
The paths may be narrow or
wide but never secular.

The future speaks to me
as a brisk wind,
clashing and fleeting
with whispers and hints.
Knowing me better than I,
lifting as I fly away.

Gatekeeper

A romanticized vision
of a vessel less solitary,
confined by brick and mortar.

The seas of green wave to me,
longing for the treacherous journey.

I shan't wallow, yet, set sail
through cataclysmic corridors.

This hollowed machines fury;
bring me life through tides wind.

Souls warmth eludes me.
A torch-less ember
abandoned in transfer,
cast down to the grip
of abysmic dwelling.

I shall not follow
nor wait for you there.
As they continue to seek, and I long,
I'll lead them to my secret room.

Growth

The world is constantly speaking
through dreams and memories.
A brighter day; this is the prospect
I've been imagining.

Look upon me with open eyes,
I'm finally shedding my disguise.

A paradoxical contemplation.
Resolve conflicting with meditation.

Eyes closed, it's your bitter end.
Hibernation is your permanent
state; you didn't begin.

Come forth to its call.
Separated from those
who seldom see all.
Before they'll let you stand,
it's filth through which you will crawl.

Hell

Stifled by his word,
I seem to recall a coarse cast
approached in bitter tongue.

Why is it I cannot see?
Where has this particle
lain lonely?

Does it not merit approach?

These depths have been dug
many centuries over.

Why have we not found the bottom?
Why aren't we searching for the top?

I do not long to battle with
his or his counters' voice any longer.
These notes transcribed
by the lowly one,
do not serve as a gate
well enough fortified.

Though I know he sees me
standing in the darkness —
I cannot tell if it's me,
or if he is smiling.

I'm Sure

As are the bridges we cross;
only when we cross them.

Identity

You speak of genius
while I ponder the level
in which I reside.

I bask in the sun
to discern my sequence.

The edge of the realm
where he exists,
I've waded.

I see now,
the pursuit is frivolous.

He is I,
and I am He.
I will remain there
on the hour written.

Though, for now,
we embark
on the perilous journey.

I imagine a road of ash
as we walk
to proclaim your power.

Please hear me
my brothers, my sisters,
you are already chosen.

"I really enjoy this piece. It's a realization I had one night, though I've had it many times before. We struggle to find meaning in nearly everything. We pray to our God(s) in hopes they hear us and grant favor for our servitude. This piece represents a message that ultimately, I want the entirety of this book to display. That being, you are what you seek."

"You are already the person you pray to be. You are already the person who has the success and prosperity you seek. You just don't know it or believe it because you have been conditioned not to. If you're anything like me, your mind is too noisy to understand."

"There is nothing wrong with praying; I do numerous times a day. I believe however, you've already been given everything you need to be the person you envision. You're here, now, and you're alive. We are God, and God is us. Not in a literal sense of course, but in the essence of the spirit we've been given."

"Understand how your mind shapes the world around you. Be aware enough to recognize when, and how you're being influenced. Cease to allow those who aim to cast you down into your life. These are some of the greatest powers we have. I think James Allen said it best, "As a man thinketh, so he shall be."

hould cons~~truct~~ delineation
of the mother's voice,
a presumed sound in
virtue and understanding.

The complexity of her
creations ~~forget~~
the limitations of their
speech and their
abundance of
sensory experience.
feel, to listen, to understand.

My children sear for their
            hearing not
~~Frequency~~ not having
realized, they seek only in
the light ~~as~~ I exist in
           yes
Shadow.

May ~~the greatest force~~ more
~~through you in effect~~ to
~~manet~~ When the deity
approaches, it may move
through you to mend and

The felicies of
our creation
suspend us in
abandoned wonderm[ent]

The selfishness to
apprehend continues
Satisfaction and
understand ~~⬛~~ ~~⬛~~
whats seeker.

The Solitude o[f]
~~the~~ storms; [the]
power and r[e]
Existence presen[t]
in fragments
7 fusion with
calice intent
avert our

The journey
as a wind
~~⬛~~ like the

Image of a Ghost

Should one's delineation
of the Mothers voice,
be presumed sound
in virtue and understanding?

The complexity of
Her creations forget the
limitations of their speech,
amidst the abundance of
sensory experience.

To feel, to listen, to
understand.

Her children scour
for their frequency.
Having not realized,
they seek only in the light,
yet, She exists in shadow.

When the deity approaches
it may move through you,
to mend and to build.

In return,
taking what is owed
in preparation for a second;
a day not given.

The fallacies of our creation
suspend us in abandoned
wonderment.

A selfishness to approbate
continual satisfaction,
with mere and bleak
understanding of what's
secular.

Thus,
there exists solace in
Her storms; power and rage.

Existence remains presented
in fragments of illusion,
cut with callus intent
to avert our gaze.

The journey appears as a
window.

As She declares the way open,
take no more than a seconds
pause. The ledge becomes you;

Jump.

Indignation

Do you beg me mindful
as I behold your callous?

Should it be
that your lips become quaint
in the shadow of your action?
Or will you remain encumbered
by the air and lie dormant?

Do not want nor follow.

The mammal consumed
by the engulfing rage
the creator has provided,
gleaming at the emissary.

Should you come to know thy will;
have it polished for you to see?

Here ,child, there is a step
before the door.

It is but one.

You have placed
your dominant side upon it.

Breathe,
the fall is looming.

It Breeds

Yes,
I hear you.

I just don't know.
I don't know.

Quiet now —
be quiet.

I never knew nothing
could be filled
with so much something.

Somethings —

these things,
these things,
these things.

I hope your pit echoes
as the wind has.

The wind
I use to wash you away.

You,
you ridiculous excuse.

Filth —
filthy as they grow.

The roots, they grow deep.

nes
{hears the call, the search, connect, misdeed}

essence, sensation, primality, ~~rebirth~~ rebirth

Kings

(1) Upon a night, skys moon full. They shall here the call.

A call name beneath shall here. It will come ~~~~ as the wind.

Should it start a whisper, they will ~~~~ regard its ressonance.

The one aside you will not wake. The glow of the flame makes way to the corridor.

(2) Through this, your first step, you may enter the room ~~to~~ from which he ~~~~ summoned you.

There, it will be revealed. These men have shared the heart numerous ...color not.

Kings

Upon a night,
skies moon full —
they shall hear the call.

A call none
beneath shall hear.
It will come as the wind.

Should it start a whisper,
you will soon regard its resonance.

The one aside you
shall not wake.
The glow of the flame
makes way to the corridor.

Through this,
you may enter the room
from which He summoned you.

Here, it will be revealed.

These men have
shaded their hearts numerous —

color not.

"Kings" was inspired by a moment I imagined meeting God. It made me realize how unique every interaction with the source is; how everyone falls short. When it's meant for you, then it shall be. You will not be given what you are not prepared for."

Love

I plead with you precious soul,
as borrowed words fall upon you,

Rise.

Scour in your dystopia no longer.
Place claim over your
perceived omnipresence.

If by choice you
intend to dwell there,
know others may reside.

There is a light you see,
that will not follow you down.

I've surrendered every ounce;
I am given only one more.
It remains bestowed upon you
through rhythm and enchantment.

You must see.
You must hear.

He has only given me salvation
for one such cause.

An everlasting journey,
forever dwelling in this ether.

I'll pick up and put together,
remaining the master of your mind,
having never known my own.

Mind

They say,
you can't lose what you never had —
but I did anyway.

Missing Her

A pain,
a pain many know.
One's light is lost,
and crushed is their soul.

She stalks as lion
in a shadow called home.
Never seeing her,
ever aware of her groan.

There she resides,
in the darkness and depths.
Footsteps into the brush,
in silence I wept.

Not by allure, but
temptation and will.
The air remains quiet now,
empty and still.

Longing for what was and
perhaps, what could have
been.

She drifts ever further now,
claimed by the sea once again.

No courage,
no strength until now.
Why must I watch her flee
to seemingly know how?

I shall be reborn, perhaps one
day. For now, adrift, forever
astray. Crippling me, a burden
to bear. She'll be greater than
I've known, without me there.

Sometimes,
we'll meet in our dreams.
Away from pain,
and the darkness of things.

Until I awake,
in silence once more.
Left with the anguish of
missing her, and
the hole that it tore.

"I had been writing for years before I started writing poetry. I filled journals with various happenings of the days, weeks, and months; no reason for it. This, however, was one of the earliest poems I had ever written. One of the first times I had ever attempted to take an emotion or series of and tie them to a structure such as this. It's rather apparent the anguish I felt over this young woman. I was very attached as a young man, and subsequently, ended up greatly hurt by its end."

"Young relationships have a habit of doing this. It's quite humorous reading it now. Neither of us had any idea what we were doing. That's to say, there were many tumultuous times between us. None of which were more her fault than mine. Ultimately, after many years of struggle, we separated for good. It was for the best. Toxic relationships make life far more difficult. Even still, I do wish her all the best in life."

"If this work makes its way into your hands, I hope you're well."

Moonlight

I spoke to myself once,
through a hole in the wall.

We had both been stuck there.

It was not with words, yet,
silence we approached.

I could fade with him.

The me sitting there,
waiting —
quiet.

We needed not noise;
we knew from whence
the other had come.

It was there,
in a moment of solidarity —
we allowed each other to live
and to die, peacefully.

Until we called to one another again,
through a hole in the wall.

Mother

There was a son
whose mother called forth.
She longed for his embrace
amidst the calamity.

It was of solemn regard
she proclaimed her intent.
Tried and true, we met there.

The field was thick
and consumed by brush.

One had nearly fallen,
for their eyes were upon us,
yet, we remained firm.

The gathering of those
who we see in shade,
made persistent the force
with which we place claim.

The voices of the wind echoed
as the mind has.
Its plains evermore
expansive with each thought.

Burrowing toward a hope
of limited understanding
and apprehensive choices,
made prior to the
closing of one's eyes.

I knew, however,
she came from the Sun.

A realm of which we may
never know.

As our colors were deemed
black, we embraced our
placement amongst the
watchers.

We see;
we listen.

The arrival of the Supreme
is too far to come,
to wallow in folly deed
any longer.

Her power grew
as she fed her longing
for resonated word.

Why would you say you're
waiting?

Can't you see?

It's always been you.

"This will be the hardest truth I share with you. My childhood wasn't what you would call, "ideal"; many aren't. Have you picked up on that yet? From a very young age, and for many years into my "young adult" life, my mother was an opioid addict and what you may call, a "working girl". This circumstance isn't unique in and of itself but, nevertheless. I honestly wasn't sure if I'd be able to share that with you, or if it was even appropriate to. My mother and I did speak about it prior. She was naturally worried about her reputation, as was I. It was understood, however, the whole story must be told."

"Truthfully speaking, it's a very important part of my story. It defined me growing up. The lifestyle we were exposed to shaped and molded me in many ways, therefore, it's necessary to share. Certainly not because I want you to pity me. Nor do I want this to seem like I'm shaming my mother. You have to understand that when a person's mind is consumed by addiction, they'll do anything to feed it. Everything about that person, and who they really are, ceases control to that addiction."

"I wouldn't change it for the world. My experiences, though many were quite rough, gave me a perspective on the world I would have never received otherwise. It gave me an insatiable drive to make an impact on people. Such as the one I'm hoping to make on you. My mother is one of the hardest working, generous people I know."

"This is dedicated to her struggle alone, as well as ours together. I love you Ma. I hope that by sharing this I don't offend or hurt you. It's important they see what's possible."

Once

Once, I awoke a man with destiny and soul.
Once, I smiled and looked upward; a day renewed.

Once, my dreams spoke to me, and I to them.
Contempt and comfortable; inspired and ambitious.

Once, I became a sick man. A man whose aura began to fade.
Once, I noticed I was cold, barren and unable to become warm.

Once, the Mother of our earth no longer rose for me.
My dreams spoke to me, but I did not understand.

Once, my soul was stolen; my face frozen and cracked.
Once, I no longer knew where I was or who surrounded me.

Demons became allies; my God lying dormant within.
Once, I leapt from the highest ledge I could find.

I was broken within and without.
Once, I climbed back up and realized.

Once,

I was in love.

"Soooo dramatic…"

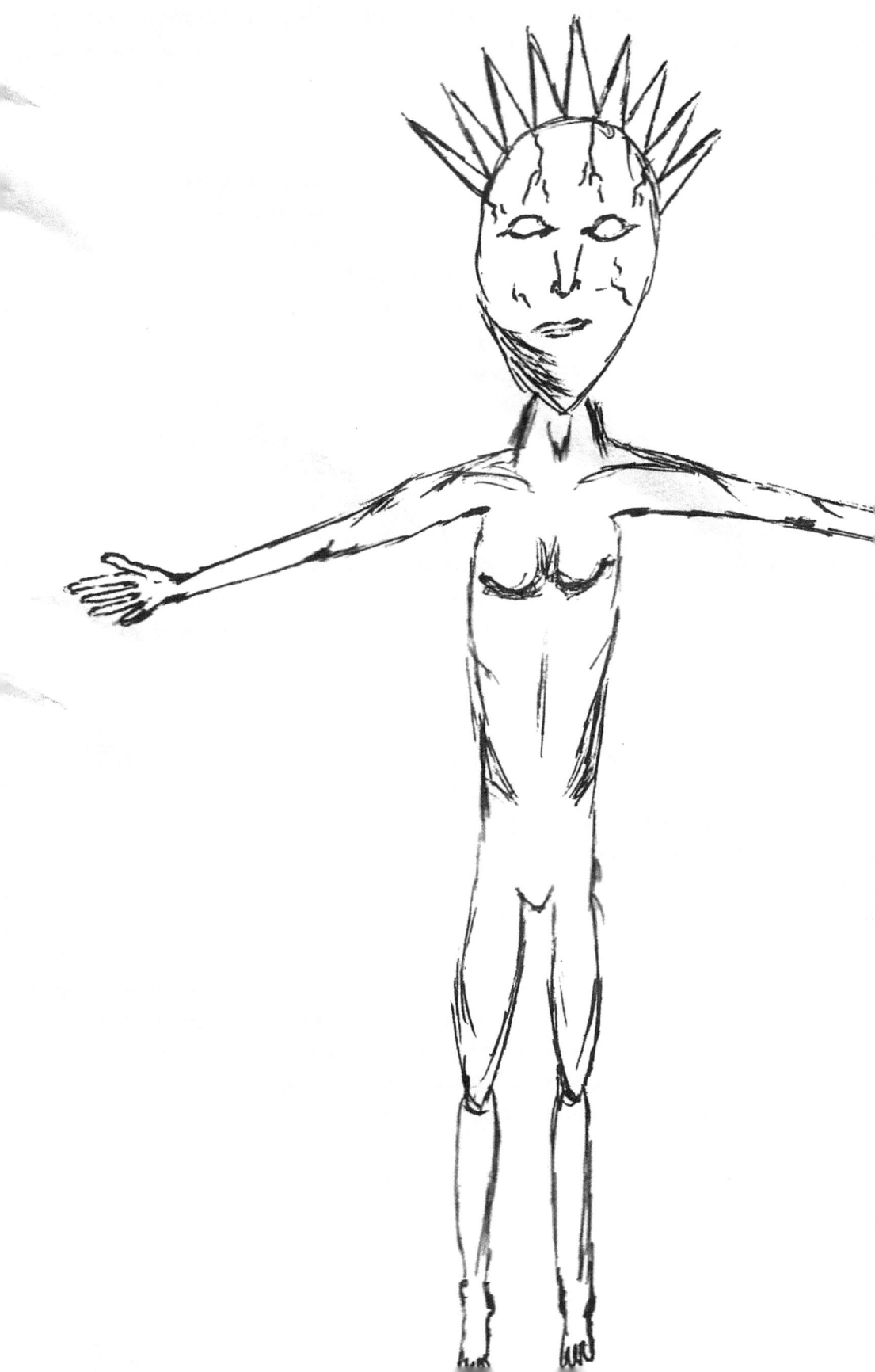

Pandora

With pins to his face
and chains abound,
his entropy began.

Crafted from their hands
with seductive intent;
power from the ancients
shaped the mold.

Such a beautiful artifact,
counseled for frail wanderings
and glazed eyes.

Gifts from scatterings
of the ruin at their feet.
A plentiful harvest,
to carry the darkest allure
of the realm below.

The depravity of man
placed assured bounty
into their hands.

As they stood
gathered around the fire,
his crown was cast
and her hands uplifted.

Peace

It's mysticism
that looms in the air.

Would you dare think
I had not longed for the call?

Covet you shall;
there is a mirage on foot.

I've seen the days grow old
as I clamor for their peace.
I am their keeper;
as the Oak stood lone.

His breath —
soon upon them;
it is the rigid we must pray for.

I guard the road I walk.
It is a wondrous place of travel.
No signs,
merely a gust beneath me.

The rain stings as it caresses.
Days —
quite beautiful.

The Path,
I have yet made it.
The road is, as the water.

Posterity

It is for you
this relic has been created.
You may keep it in
your labyrinth for solace.

Do you see yourself reflected,
as you indulge in idealized
synchronies within the ether?

I see you there
amongst the mystics.

You, however,
remain fragmented.
Not permitted to retain
the relevance you posses.

As you exist in shade,
so you shall remain.

Conflicted by the light of the
Sun, and the voice of the
Moon, we'll embrace you
as you awake from your slumber.

Prairie

The sound reverberated
through the aura.
As the eye of this realm
illuminates their hands,
a firm gaze is fixed above.

Never has one seen so clearly
than with eyes closed.
The ears of these creations
have heard the rhythm of the soul,
one that is warm and like no other.

We exist on the riverbed
as we do in the atmos;
never having come nor gone.
Breathing deepest,
just before the last is taken.

Should you be given the choice
at your time of awakening,
please do share the stories
of your many ventures here.

Puppet Master

May I access what lies within?
Should I want to know
the dark corridors of His home?

I've resided there,
as many have before.
It must warrant merit.

Though I know
His face sheds smile nor frown.
His tears only fall
when I need them.

Amidst the tyranny
you proclaim faith
in minuscule victory,
eluding to what one
knows means nothing.

Perhaps in nothing,
I'll find his key.
She holds it for me
in His dark place.

Purgatory

For a moon or many,
I may wake nor sleep at all
amidst his grasp.

The Shadows I'd never long for,
nestled in every corner.

My eyes may continue to fixate
on the void in front of me.

I've granted him a
conceded sacrifice.

So, it is we who have fallen
and been stripped of our wings.

I cling to the faintest glimmer,
as I crawl my way back.

Purpose

The moon's mask
places claim on the air.

A solitary time fade
encapsulated in pragmatic
occurrences, reflecting
such a shining spectacle.

The tides ebb and flow,
mirroring stolen fragments
of sacrificed vitality.

Oh, our most bitter heave,
and most grueling hoe.

Emblematic realizations,
of lessons lived and learned
through vicarious souls prior.

To these words we cling;
to these lessons we heed.

Motionless memory formatted
for transcendental travel.
Eclectic offerings and tithes,
through which a vessel
is made whole by the
greatest of dwellings.

Loathing apprehension,
bound by chains on the
edges brink, pulled by the
Master's hand to heavenly
bodies above.

Made to rise in noble causes
and actions next to fear.
My adversary's downfall
beckons on the horizon.

The new day has come forth
with wholesome offerings in
hand, outstretched and eager
for embrace.

Bound by greater instinct
and virtue, than the man
led by the dog.

May a plethora of knowledge
and carnal fire, be brought up
and immortalized through the
Creator's most righteous and
divine of beings.

The dawn approaches over
this, the mightiest of storms.

I awaited his call,
and now stand firmly ashore.

Rain

Irony is the weather
filling my head.
That of which
I long for the most.

To see its face.
The brightest of days
made dark by its haunting allure.

The tremble and scream
of its frustration and power.
Cracking its whip
as a flood upon the earth.

Swaying from side to side
what stands tall and firm.
Allowing these beings to remain;
casting down those it preys upon.

We beckon its approach
with sirens and dread,
as it brings to life
what was once dead.
Perhaps it's no coincidence,
this rain is filling my head.

"For as long as I can remember, I've had a fascination with storms, coastal storms especially. There's something about the atmosphere of a strong storm that always seems to grab my attention and hold it. Though I know they can be dangerous, I've never found them threatening. Perhaps it's related to the tone the poem describes."

"That being, I often feel it's a stormy mess in my head. I suppose I relate to the chaos of such a day. Oh geez...I really am a poet...."

River

Swim to the bottom.
You —
swim.

Release to the undertow;
a current unknown.

You must watch slowly,
as the depths become you.

It is for your attention
you are cold here.

As you realize
you've made it below,
you will awaken.

Sun scorched eyes shall behold,
You —
In the ripple below your brow.

Your gasp released —
water clear.

Swim You —
swim.

Salvation

I found on the horizon
the offering you shan't accept.

No worry need be placed
if my extension to accept
this peril aids my fellow brethren.

To think of shame
how I've seen you.
To understand the sorrow
how you've seen me.

Could you take
the travelers endured message
and culminate a man?

You place a call to kneel,
as vessels scream
from hollowed divinity.

Is it not enough
we mask the floor
in blood and tear?

We shed a skin
in hopes of you're
acceptance and call;
just as the rabbit asked us to follow.

Singularity

It seems one may have
seen the great divide.
A desolate paradise
given at favor.

Chemical saturation
voids the barrier,
leaving one to
contemplate the steps taken.

The melody of silence
gives glimpse to such
pieces removed; such gained.

Suspended in motion,
one ponders if His
hand will be extended.

Sorry

I no longer wish to be.

So wearisome
the need —
the need to be.

I no longer wish to wonder.

How loud it is
this silence.

For what I may achieve;
perhaps not —

I no longer wish to be.

Succession

He had once given me a mirror.
I pointed it to the sun
to guide a traveler home.

It was reflected in the water
placed in his hand.

Seen only as a prism,
he remained suspended.

The view of the valley
remained encumbered
by the opening of the gate.

His brother below
aggregated his shape.

How could it be,
he saw so well from his peak,
yet, only felt in slumber?

This piece was made for him.

Sitting on the altar before him,
it beckoned the answer.
As he drank from the fountain,
he awoke alone in his cell.

Suicide

She awoke alone in the cellar,
unaware of how she arrived
there.

She noticed she was
unable to move.
It was dark —
cold.

From a place above,
water splashed against
her face;
it did not relieve her.

Her eyes scan the room.
A figure there —
the corner,
in the darkness.

Petrified,
she dare not move,
even if she could.

The figure —
from shadow,
began to approach her
absent of sound,
as if it didn't move at all.

She closed her eyes;
counted the beats of her heart
like a drum inside her.

He knelt.

She could feel his presence
as he lowered to her ear,
"I can help you,"
he said.

When she opened her eyes,
the ground didn't seem so far
away.

"Suicide, in this generation, has become a significant problem. The majority of our music is blatant with thoughts and/or feelings of depression, and suicide. The same can be said for a lot of our media. People continually trying to cope with their loss of self; how fragile our identity is. Even those we wouldn't expect to see fall do as well. "They have it all", we say."

"I'm not sure what it is, about the time we live in, that's caused so many people to choose this fate for themselves. I've struggled with bouts of depression many times before; suicidal thoughts were certainly a part of that."

"In a way, I admire those who choose to take their own life. I can imagine how that must sound to you. I, however, believe it takes a tremendous amount of courage. You are permanently ending an existence; your existence, having no clue what's to come. That, of course, is not to say that I in any way glorify or encourage it. The amount of mental pain and anguish an individual goes through, causing them to end their life, is undoubtedly great."

"This poem was inspired by those who have struggled with those feelings, either past or present. I believe It's very important we take a hard look at what's causing this problem. What does it say about the world we live in?"

The Brotherhood

Should it be that
the corners of the room
were made of three instead of four.

That the light from the center
should be above or below.

The hidden mass
of universal answer;
of mystics and alchemists,
wielding the magic of the elders.

The shroud rests lightly.
A blade to my chest
and a call to kneel
conclude my initiation.

To live or to perish,
it has not been deemed,
for I have yet to see
His art before me.

The Good Shepard

The tool I wield
obtains no merit;
no reward.

You observe a
shimmer in the sand.

He screams to me
to attain the power of His realm.
I place claim for you there.

The gestation of this offering,
eclipsed by hieroglyphic translation.

I smile as the soil births
your planted seed.

He reminds me of how it
must grow; how I must
remain its keeper.

The Grey

It's the search.
Why you wander
during the day.
Why I cannot
sleep at night.

The Search —
oh, our symbols,
how precious they are.

I don't mind
how high you've
suspended your halo.

Our words in exchange
draw us nearer
to the source.

The Less You Say

Shall I remove my voice
from the proverbial fray,
or alter its tone for a distant day.

Shall they remain inside,
words not spoken.
To ponder a lesson,
these breaths were chosen.

So loud you won't hear,
off fierce ridges they bounce.
It seems my tone recollects me,
I haven't spoken an ounce.

The Marked Ones

They must see so beautifully.
It is not a destination
but the stone behind;
a glimpse of one to come.

A foot planted
as a flower amidst the soil.

You are released here.
With continual lesson,
you will seek.

Your separation may
blur your vision —
perfectly complete,
still you seek.

Do not fear the answer unknown.
You'll realize when you've come to see,
the blade of grass is the roar of your soul.

The Skeleton Key

Could it be so true,
that a cataclysm
such as this would align.

That a Spirit
may have appended itself
to my dwelling.

Frustrations and curses of
ages-old, demand reprimand
for your cost and penalty.

I scorn the thought of your reprieve.

As if you move Creature,
to violate sanctity, yet,
I'm left to wonder why I'm
still on my knees in front of you.

The box remains open.
Ten thousand days;
stake in hand.

The Voyage

It's not just you
that's seen the light fade.

I'll simply always be,
a thousand miles away.

It's now a time, when
timeless times seem timeless
now.

When ~~the~~ inescapable degredations
loom as shadows only
deunted by carnal
endeavors relentlessly
pursued.

~~It's~~ happiness demands
our explanations
as if ~~@@@@@@@~~ we harness
~~@@@@@@@~~ happiness's explanation
whilst we claim and
seek it, to and
fro; those promises
we offer as
charitable terms.

I do not know I nor trust.
Yet strive forwards demands
made by thine self
and the greater's lesson and bow

This Masterful Ceremony shared
by those rich with garments
of soiled rags; ~~@@@~~

Time

It's now seen clear,
the illusion of the infinite.

Inescapable degradation
looms as shadow,
only daunted by carnal
endeavors relentlessly pursued.

Happiness demands
our explanations,
as if we harness
happiness's explanation.

Whilst we claim and seek it,
to and fro. Those empty
promises we offer as
charitable tokens.

I do not know I nor trust, yet,
strive towards demands
made by thine self and the
Master's lesson and journey.

This masterful ceremony,
shared by those rich
with garments of soiled rag.
Coercing with hollowed
vessels of vice and disdain,
kneeling before
golden statues erected.

But one pursuit
should come to fruition.
Manifested by the calamity
of unknown entities power
discerned.

Propelled by ungraspable
hourglass moments,
as I reach for his hand
and long for his face.

Tomorrow

It's morning now,
the day is great.
Cooking breakfast —
perhaps I'll wait.

A shower now,
to clear my head.
Silence abound,
the air is dead.

To the room,
I'm wide awake.
To make the bed —
perhaps I'll wait.

I'm older now,
much more aware.
I wonder what's been waiting,
way over there.

Perhaps a new skill,
or another first date.
Today, I take a stand —
perhaps I'll wait.

A life long-lived.
A long life alive.
The machines ring loud,
what a good day to die.

One more meal,
a happy clean plate.

Yes,
what a good day to die —
perhaps I'll wait.

"Tomorrow", at its core, is a poem about procrastination. I'm one of the worst when it comes to this. "You only get one life to live", as they say. You should be working but shouldn't work it away. Do what you can to better yourself. Become the best version of you that you possibly can. What conversations do you have with yourself? This is one of mine."

Transmigration

To heaven above
from earth below,
I've pleaded and sworn.

Lived as the devil,
to live without evil.

Guided has been thy hand;
thy body.
Heart lost and soul tired,
scowled by the intricacies
of divination.

Even still,
amidst the juxtaposition,
I've arrived there —
a clearing.

A once cursed man
with bitter word on sliver
tongue,
hast now brought forth
and eternity of vision.

The voice I longed to hear so
often,
had never remained silent.
It was the word
I bled into the paper.

The perpetual light,
freely given to vessels
lost in the night.

The tumultuous road
paved with sorrow, fear, and
pride.
A man's spirit which he did
not claim,
yet, he clamored to keep.
Now washed with gold and
silver,
beckoning a momentous
arrival.

My son,
it has always been you.

You are here,
forgiven and solidified
in the ever-present
essence of serenity.

With an abundance of word
from loose lips past;
teeth seldom omnipotent.
I look forward to resting
thine ear of you,
as you receive the word from
me.

Twelve

What if it was taken?
This crystalline sphere
in its entirety.
Immortalized encapsulation
of woe released and uplifted.

Such plunder the approbation,
given from folly of thought.
The heart he gave to his Majestic,
may now lie forever dormant.

The visions he placed
between the ripple,
bestow their detriment
to the fondest of longings.

The sky has been shaded
with one's nomadic demeanor.
I've received the glass,
within which my futility beckoned.

He called to me.
Spoke as if I were
one of his own.
The masquerade allotted me
the most elegant of faces.
Still, I did not enter.

I rested aside a snake
while the dove sang to me.
Called forth,
I was to rise exactly where I stood.

Veil

Could you ask me the poison
of my choice and gain clarity?

You hadn't understood
a moments passing
before reading a word written.

Those lingering
may pass beneath you
for minute offerings,
as you remain secular and weary.

I hope you bury yourself
on His occasion.
His face will become
familiar to you prior.

You seem to me as a shade,
and henceforth,
she'll be waiting for you
below the garden.

Vessels

If I were to speak of feeling,
you may believe I possessed it.

Eyes locked,
of which, contain worlds
amidst collision.

Perhaps as day breaks,
we'll set forth together.

Until then,
you remain a glimmer.

Refractions we should
hope to cling to.

I'll smile as the dopamine fades.

Can you tell me my name?

Void

Is it the seclusion
that calls you forth?

Are you only visible
in the shade which you exist?

The Creator
must hang a head heavy
at your cognizance.

Blessed are those
who see without sight.

To be simple.
To be pure.

Can you feel the wind;
hear their call?

This is I;
It is you.

Do not fret,
I am waiting.

Wave

Briskly it goes by,
so briskly it goes by.

I don't believe they'd see
a ripple such as I.

Here in the middle,
oh here —
in the middle.

I wonder if, before I die,
they'll see a ripple like me
as they pass briskly on by.

"All I've ever felt for certain was that I needed to impact people. Somehow, I needed to share a story; my story. I feel many of us long for this, especially those who choose to create in any capacity. We have this "thing" within us we don't quite understand but know it's there for something bigger than ourselves. Hopefully, this work has in some way, impacted you."

You Should Rest...

You needn't worry, nor have I;
I've been sleeping for a very long time.

-Epilogue-

"I hope you've enjoyed your time here with me, as I have sharing these stories with you. This is my soul, my ghosts, the experiences and visions it holds. Well, at least the first collection of that is. Though I explained the meaning and inspiration behind some of these poems, I hope you're able to derive some meaning and familiarity in the ones I did not. I told myself when I began writing, that this would be it for this chapter of my life; that I would take the entirety of my first 26 years here and give it away. It's a candid, honest account, and it means more for you to have it than I."

"It's important to note again, that my story and struggle is not unique. This work was not meant to emphasize struggle simply for the sake of struggle however, I do want you to understand what you can make it through. I, along with my sister, was pulled from school at a very young age. We moved around quite a bit. It became quite hard to maintain steady friends or people to rely on. My family usually viewed my sister and me as the black sheep, the outcasts. That isn't to say they were completely void from our lives, more-so, the actions of our parents simply fell on our shoulders."

"My father, during the latter half of our lives, became an addict as well. At one low point, he attempted to end his life. He was found in the front seat of his car after he had taken a blade to himself."

"Today, I'm just a young man who's had to face his demons by any means I was able. Believe me when I say it wasn't easy. I'm blessed in numerous ways though; many I don't deserve. My sister has two healthy children, and my mother is in a far better place in life."

"My father is at least alive, breathing, and working. Unfortunately, he wasn't a very prominent part of my life; as a father figure that is. I love my father, but he never taught me how to be a man. Though, I suppose he did the best he could. I do love you though dad, and I wish the best for you."

"The trials you are put through in life don't simply happen. They are meant to teach you something. To prepare you for a higher level of knowledge and understanding. You can overcome anything and would be a fool to believe you won't be tested. That's all this life is. You'll be much happier in the end if you're able to understand, there is no point. The only reason you're alive is to be just that; alive. Everything we can add on top of that is just icing on the cake."

"Now that all this doom and gloom is over, I do look forward to sharing more of my life with you in the future. A better, more matured life. Believe in yourself relentlessly, and never let someone tell you your dreams aren't worth fighting for. They are the only thing worth fighting for. Accept yourself and your flaws, but always strive for growth."

"Do not let your mind fall victim. Keep your faith and never give up. Aim to serve something bigger than yourself. It took me 26 years to get here. It took my whole life's experience to write these poems. Trust the process and never lose sight of who you are. I'm a poet, pretending to be a painter, but mostly just a man."

"Until we speak again..."

- Chaz Allen

Acknowledgements

"I'd like to thank everyone who's listened to me talk about this project month, after month...after month and kept supporting me; my friends, my loved ones, and especially my family."

"To everyone I've shared a piece of my story or work with; everyone who can relate to the motivation behind the struggles we face."

"To anyone who simply opened to the first page of this book. Thank you."

Author Bio

Chaz Allen McQuerrey, otherwise known as "Chaz Allen", is an American poet based in Chattanooga, Tennessee. His journey with writing began at a very early age, but he did not venture into poetry until he was around 16; this is where he found his home in writing. Chaz's poems are often wrapped in allegory, metaphor, abstraction, and span a wide variety of subjects to convey a deeper message than one may expect to find on the surface alone.

With the release of *The Thirteenth Circle*, Chaz marks his entry into the world of published literature. His first collection of poems aims to invoke a truly visceral response from its readers. The autobiographical nature of its writing, along with the details shared, undoubtedly beg the reader to dig deeper.

REACH OUT AND CONNECT WITH ME!

www.ChazAllenArt.com

ChazAllenArt

BE SURE AND LEAVE A REVIEW!

www.ingramcontent.com/pod-product-compliance
Lightning Source LLC
Chambersburg PA
CBHW062027290426
44108CB00025B/2814